Sky Pony Press books may be purchased in bulk at special discounts for sales promotion,
corporate gifts, fund-raising, or educational purposes. Special editions can also be created
to specifications. For details, contact the Special Sales Department, Sky Pony Press,
307 West 36th Street, 11th Floor, New York, NY 10018 or info@skyhorsepublishing.com.
Sky Pony® is a registered trademark of Skyhorse Publishing, Inc.®,
a Delaware corporation.

Visit our website at www.skyponypress.com.

10 9 8 7 6 5 4 3 2 1

Manufactured in China, October 2023
This product conforms to CPSIA 2008

Library of Congress Cataloging-in-Publication Data is available on file.

Cover design by Elke Kohlmann & Kai Texel
Cover illustrations by Nikolai Renger
US Edition edited by Nicole Frail

Print ISBN: 978-1-5107-7707-1
Ebook ISBN: 978-1-5107-7708-8

Don't Stress About Stress

Tips and Exercises for Everyday Life

Written by
Dagmar Geisler

Illustrated by
Nikolai Renger

Translated by
Andy Jones Berasaluce

Sky Pony Press
New York

Table of Contents

Stress for Kaleb

Kaleb holds his breath. He doesn't really want to listen, but he can't ignore it either.

The voices belong to Hannah and Joe. They've hidden in the bushes next to the gymnasium. Kaleb was only trying to look for the ball that Mila shot wide for the thousandth time.

"We have to do something," says Hannah in a sullen voice.

Joe says, just as sullenly, "Yeah, otherwise it'll ruin everything."

Kaleb winces. Are they talking about him?

Why wouldn't they be? He *was* the one who had broken Hannah's water bottle, the pretty one with the golden dolphins. But that hadn't been on purpose! Plus, he'd apologized.

"We'll end it," Hannah scoffs. Kaleb gulps.

"Well, how are we going to do that?" asks Joe.

"First, let's write down everything we know. Then we'll see what happens next," Hannah says aggressively.

"Good," says Joe. "Let's meet up in your garden! This afternoon at about three?"

Kaleb's nose itches. He can't sneeze now! He crawls backward quietly.

"Where have you been?" calls Mila.

She'd found the ball somewhere else long ago.
The game continues.

Now it's Kaleb who keeps shooting the ball wrong.
"What's the matter with you?" asks Mila.

The Soda–Candy Conspiracy

Hannah's family's garden plot is within a community garden. Kaleb knows where it is, and he has been there several times, most recently for Hannah's birthday party. That was in the spring.

Now, everything looks very different. Huge plants and pumpkins are growing everywhere. And have there always been so many paths? Which one leads to Hannah's garden?

9

It takes him a while to find his way through the maze. But now he recognizes everything: The bright blue shed. The curtains with dots on the windows. The tree with the swing. And the pink doghouse.

Metzger the dog is there, too.

But Kaleb isn't afraid. After all, he wants to find out what those two know about him. Have they figured out that his uncle doesn't play baseball in the big leagues at all, but rather for the local minor team in town?

Metzger, which is the German word for "butcher," lies lazily in the sun, occasionally twitching his floppy ear. The two kids in the garden shed probably think he'll bark when someone's coming.

But what dog barks after being fed the finest organic sausage? (Especially one named after a butcher!) Kaleb swiped some from the fridge at home—a whole ring of sweet sausage. Metzger is very excited and lets Kaleb sneak past without a sound. Kaleb quickly scurries behind the shed.

A lot of junk is stored in there. That's good. He can easily find a place to hide if someone suddenly approaches.

At the back of the shed is a large window. It's open a crack. "Perfect!" thinks Kaleb. He'll be able to hear everything they say.

Carefully, he peeks inside. The two are sitting at the table and drinking bright pink sodas with candies fizzing in their cups.

"Well," Hannah says. "We have most of it, unless you can think of anything else?" She taps the paper with her pen.

Joe shakes his head and slurps loudly through his straw. Then he says, "Read it out loud!"

Kaleb moves a little closer to the window. Nice! He arrived just in time.

Down to the Wire

RRRROOOOWWWWW!

It's Metzger. Oh man, is his bark loud! A real bloodcurdling howl. Hannah and Joe jump up, startled. A chair tips over, and pink bubbles splash across the room.

The two run out the front door after Metzger. The dog runs out of the garden, barking loudly, and follows a black furball with ears.

Oh no! The beast stole the sausage!

Kaleb sees his chance. He throws the window open all the way, jumps into the shed, grabs the list, and in a flash, is out again. Good job, Metzger!

The List

Kaleb would love to get out of the garden right away. But what if he runs straight into the others? Instead, he hides for the moment in a giant plastic shell that used to be a sandbox. There's no sand in it anymore, just lots of old toys.

Kaleb props an old bucket under the lid to get some air. A bit of light comes in with the air, enough to read what Hannah and Joe wrote about him.

Totally wears you out!

Really?

Constantly causes trouble!

But he knew that.

Hits people in the stomach!

Lies!

Devours people alive!

Kaleb gasps. They're completely crazy. And there's more.
Things just keep getting worse and worse.

Makes it so Daddy can't sleep.

Responsible for Mom's headache.

The reason why our custodian at school had to go to the hospital.

With flashing lights and wailing sirens!

"Oh, gosh!" Kaleb exclaims and covers his mouth in shock. That was too loud. Hopefully no one heard. . . . Too late.

Whoosh! The lid of the shell flies open.

"What are you doing in here?" Hannah calls out. And a black, woolly something flies in Kaleb's face.

ARF! ARF! ARF! it yelps. And

WOOF! WOOF! WOOF! barks Metzger.

And Whose Fault Is That?

It took quite a while for Kaleb to free himself from the shell. Joe put a bandage on his bruised cheek. And Hannah ran to the water fountain to get Kaleb a glass of water to calm down.

It took a while for the two of them to squeeze the whole story out of him.

"Huh?" says Joe. "You really think we wrote this about you?" he asks and points to the crumpled paper in Kaleb's hand.

"Didn't you?" asks Kaleb. He feels pretty silly. "You said, 'We'll end it!' And I thought . . ."

"Seriously?" Hannah bursts out laughing.

Joe, giggling, gasps for air. "Nah," he says. "You're a little strange, but we don't want to end you." He gives Kaleb a friendly punch on the side.

"Oh man," Hannah laughs, holding her stomach. "My water bottle wasn't that nice anyway."

And then the two explain what they really want to get rid of.

Stress.

"Stress?" asks Kaleb.

"Yes," Hannah explains. "We've had enough of it. It impacts everyone. When the custodian was picked up, Mrs. Schwan said:

'Stress is to blame.'

And when Mom gets her bad headaches, she says:

'The stress is eating away at me.'"

"Sometimes my daddy can't sleep because of it, and then he's in a bad mood. And Aunt Rosie says:

'Stress hits me in the stomach,'"

recounts Joe.

"And yesterday we heard on the news:

'Stress affects our children, too,'"

says Hannah. "We have to do something!"

"What, then?" asks Kaleb.

"I have no idea," Hannah says and sighs. "We don't even know where to find it."

"Or what it even is," says Joe.

What We'd Like to Know

What exactly is stress?

Hannah, Joe, and Kaleb have become stress researchers. And now Mila has joined them.

The first thing they did was keep a tally. Every time the word stress came up, they marked a line.

> RESULTS:
> Grown-ups say the word "stress" quite often.

They also wrote down sentences in which the word appears.

> RESULTS:
> Supposedly, stress is to blame for a lot of things. Even Mrs. Gartner's pug is recently looking like a pressed sausage!

Secondly, they thought about the people they knew to see if there was someone who could help. That's when they came across Mila's Aunt Judith. She's a therapist, and she helps people avoid getting sick due to stress.

RESULTS:

1. Stress really exists.
2. You can't see it.
3. Stress is a condition in the body.
4. It occurs when you have too much to do or when something significant is going on—a commotion, for example, or an argument that cannot be resolved.
5. The body then adjusts to the fact that it now has to do a lot quickly and has to be more attentive than usual.
6. When stressed, the body is on alert:
   * The heart beats faster.
   * The breath quickens.
   * The blood flows faster through the veins.
   * Some people get red-faced.

That's actually quite normal.

Stress doesn't usually make you sick.
It's part of life.

But if you have too much of it, it's no longer healthy. This is also
the case with many other things.

For example, chocolate and gummy bears make you sick if you
eat too much of them all the time.

Stress is a condition for unusual situations. If you have it too
often, it's not healthy.

Does good stress exist?

It does.

Anything unusual puts a lot of stress on the body. It doesn't matter what.

It all blows over eventually—usually, after all the exertion, comes some relief.

This relief is good for your mind and body.

How do you know when you're stressed?

The four researchers did a survey and got many different answers:

And how can you tell if stress is becoming harmful?

The four of them discussed this question again with Mila's Aunt Judith because that's what she knows about best.

When you feel like you can't take a break because you have too much work to do.

 When you think about the things you really need to get done before going to sleep.

 When you sleep badly because of it, waking up over and over again.

 When you eat something out of sheer stress, even though you're not hungry. Or when you forget to eat and drink.

 When you no longer notice stress-related pain, even though it's there; for example, if you have a headache or your back pinches.

 It's detrimental to our health when the stressful state just doesn't stop.

What can we do to prevent stress from harming us?

Kaleb, Mila, Hannah, and Joe want to answer this question for themselves. They look back at the information they've gathered on the subject and form some ideas on their own.

One afternoon, in Hannah's garden shed, they compile all the ideas into a list.

The Anti-Stress List

 We can never forget that every job requires breaks. During the breaks, we should do something that feels different from work. If we work sitting down, the break is a chance to move around: some dancing maybe, or a bit of running, kicking around a soccer ball, or a walk around the block with Metzger.

 Movement that is fun is a great way to reduce stress. Fresh air is important, by the way.

 We shouldn't put off homework until the last moment. Otherwise, we won't have a chance to take breaks.

 If we're tired, we should rest first and not waste time with television or computer games. Those can make you even more exhausted without you noticing it right away.

 If it's all getting to be too much for us, we'll say so. Maybe something or someone else will help. Nobody can do everything!

 When the stress comes from being in a fight with someone, we should try to work it out. We can also ask for help.

 No matter what you may have to do, you must always leave time to play or relax.

 We need lots of good jokes. Laughter is good for stress.

They show the list to Aunt Judith. She thinks the ideas they collected are great. And she has another tip that helps immediately in stressful situations:

Inhale and exhale.

"Doesn't everyone always do that anyway?" asks Kaleb.

"Yes," says Aunt Judith, "but that's automatic."

Then she shows them how to breathe away stress.

This action is always possible, even when there's no time for a real break. For example, when you're taking a test at school and can't leave your desk or the room.

Sit or stand up straight.

Place your hands loosely on your stomach, directly below your ribs. Close your eyes and breathe in deeply and exhale very slowly, until all the air is out of your lungs.

Think about nothing other than how the fresh air flows into your body and how the stale air leaves you.

Feel your stomach rise and fall as you do this. Is the air you breathe in cooler than the air you breathe out? With every breath, fresh energy enters your body.

If we pay attention to all of this, stress doesn't stand a chance. It shrinks and shrinks.

Ruff! goes Metzger.

"What are we going to research next?" asks Kaleb.

Information Centers

Help Is Available:
- Family doctor or school social services
- School psychologist
- Family counseling centers in your area

National Mental Health Hotline
1-800-950-6264

National Youth Crisis Hotline
(800) 442-HOPE (4673)

National Child Traumatic Stress Initiative (NCTSI)
240-276-1310
NCTSI@SAMHSA.gov

New York
The Child Center of New York
718-651-7770
info@childcenterny.org

Cohen Family Wellness Center
43-08 52nd Street, Second Floor
Woodside, NY 11377

Jamaica Family Wellness Center
163-18 Jamaica Avenue,
Second Floor
Jamaica, NY 11432

Macari Family Wellness Center
140-15B Sanford Avenue,
Second Floor
Flushing, NY 11355

California
CalFam Counseling
16830 Ventura Boulevard, Suite 216
Encino, CA 91436
818-907-9980

Child and Family Guidance Center
9650 Zelzah Avenue
Northridge, CA 91325
818-993-9311
www.childguidance.org

Florida
Center for Child Counseling
8895 N Military Trail #300C
Palm Beach Gardens, FL 33410
561-244-9499
info@centerforchildcounseling.org

Texas
Child and Family Resource Clinic
Matthews Hall Annex
1180 Union Circle
Denton, TX 76203
940-565-2066

Afterword

Stress used to be something that only concerned adults. At least that's what people thought. But it has long been clear to everyone how much children can also suffer from the consequences of stress.

A certain amount of it is part of life. Positive stress definitely exists. But too much of it is not healthy, for the body nor for the soul.

"Alternate" is the magic word in this context. Alternating between:

* tension and relaxation,
* concentration and distraction,
* sitting still and moving,
* breathing in and breathing out.

If you pay attention to this, you're on the right track. Nevertheless, there are external circumstances that affect us so much that we can no longer get rid of the negative stress. Then it's time to get help.

The sooner, the better.

Dagmar Geisler

40

Dagmar Geisler has already supported several generations of parents in accompanying their children through emotionally difficult situations. Through her series Emotional Development for Elementary School Students, the author sensitively deals with the most important issues related to growing up: from body awareness to exploring one's own emotional world to social interactions. Her work always includes a helping of humor. Even when things get serious—then even more so.

Her books have been translated into twenty languages and also published in the USA.

Nikolai Renger was born in Karlsruhe and studied visual communication at the HFG in Pforzheim. He works as a freelance illustrator for various publishers and agencies and has been working at Atelier Remise Karlsruhe since 2013.